HMH | **English**

D0809616

LANGUAGE
LAUNCH

TABLE OF CONTENTS

Welcome to the *Language Launch*

Take this survey to preview the Issues. After each Issue, check back to see if your ideas about the topic have changed.

1: Are You Your Name?

How do you feel about your name?
Check all that apply or write your own idea.

☐ I like my name.

☐ I do not like my name.

☐ My name is an important part of who I am.

☐ I want to change my name.

☐ _____

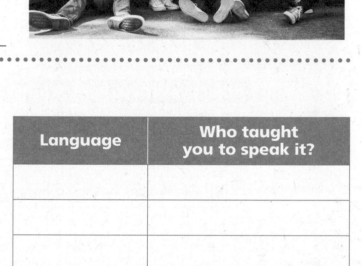

2: Keeping Languages Alive

What languages do you speak?
Who taught you to speak each language?

Language	Who taught you to speak it?

3: Your Brain and Language

What do you know about your brain and language?
Write **T** for true and **F** for false.

_____ There are separate parts of your brain for each language you know.

_____ Your brain gets bigger when you learn a new language.

_____ There is a limit to how many languages your brain can learn.

ARE **YOU** YOUR **NAME?**

Activate Knowledge

💡 BRAINSTORM IDEAS
Brainstorm precise words to complete the frame.

Question: How do you describe yourself?

Frame: I describe myself as _____ (**adjective:** *kind*)
because I _____ (**present-tense verb:** *help* . . .).

▶ I describe myself as <u>funny</u> because I <u>tell stories and make people laugh</u>.

▶ I describe myself as <u>curious</u> because I <u>like to learn about new topics</u>.

🎯 Grammar Target
An **adjective** describes or adds detail about a noun.
quick   easy   happy   tall

Adjectives (describing words)			Verbs (action words)	
intelligent	helpful	athletic	help	play
friendly	creative	serious	like to	know how to

I describe myself as _____ (adjective) . . .	because I _____ (present-tense verb . . .).
• _____	• _____
• _____	• _____
• _____	

✏️ WRITE IDEAS
Select your two favorite ideas and write complete sentences.

Language to COMPARE
My idea is like yours.
My idea is like (Name)'s.

1. _____

_____

2. _____

_____

Academic Vocabulary

BUILD WORD KNOWLEDGE
Complete the meanings and examples for the academic words.

Language to SHARE IDEAS

Which idea did you add?

I added _____.

Word	Meaning	Picture and Examples
1 **identity** i • **den** • ti • ty *noun* _____ _____	who a _____ is and what is important to them _____ 🌐	1. One part of this woman's **identity** is that she likes to _____ (base verb . . .) _____ 2. One part of my **identity** as a student is that I _____ (present-tense verb . . .) _____
2 **pronounce** pro • **nounce** *verb* _____ _____	to _____ words correctly _____ 🌐	1. The dad teaches his daughter to **pronounce** _____ (adjective) words. 2. It is important to **pronounce** words correctly when you _____ (present-tense verb . . .)
3 **affect** a • **ffect** *verb* _____ _____	to _____ someone or something _____ 🌐	1. When students study for tests, it can **affect** their _____ (noun) 2. The weather might **affect** what you decide to _____ (base verb . . .)
4 **culture** cul • ture *noun* _____ _____	the way of life that a group of _____ share 🌐	1. In Latin American **culture**, the food can be _____ (adjective) 2. Something I like about my **culture** is that we _____ (present-tense verb . . .)

Activate Knowledge

💡 BRAINSTORM IDEAS
Brainstorm precise words to complete the frame.

Question: What do you like or dislike about your name or nickname?

Frame: I (like/dislike) that my (name/nickname) is _____ (**adjective:** *short . . .*).

> ▶ I <u>like</u> that my <u>name</u> is <u>common in my culture</u>.
> ▶ I <u>dislike</u> that my <u>name</u> is <u>long and takes time to write</u>.
> ▶ I <u>like</u> that my <u>nickname</u> is <u>unique because I am the only one with my name</u>.

Adjectives (describing words)				
long	common	easy to say	popular	special
short	uncommon	difficult to say	unique	personal

👍 I like that my (name/nickname) is _____ (adjective . . .).	👎 I dislike that my (name/nickname) is _____ (adjective . . .).
• _____	• _____
• _____	• _____
• _____	• _____
• _____	• _____

✏️ WRITE IDEAS
Select your two favorite ideas and write complete sentences.

Language to COMPARE

My idea is like yours.

My idea is like (Name)'s.

1. _____

2. _____

Academic Vocabulary

BUILD WORD KNOWLEDGE
Complete the meanings and examples for the academic words.

Language to SHARE IDEAS
Which idea did you add?
I added _____.

Word	Meaning	Picture and Examples
1 **tradition** tra • **di** • tion *noun* _____ _____	something that people have done the same way for a _____ time	1. For many people, it is a **tradition** to _____ (base verb) on New Year's Eve. 2. One **tradition** I celebrate every year is _____ (noun)
2 **legacy** leg • a • cy *noun* _____	the _____ people have of someone's life	1. When people do _____ (adjective) things, they leave a good **legacy**. 2. One way to have a strong **legacy** is to _____ (base verb . . .)
3 **embarrassed** em • **bar** • rassed *adjective* _____	when others make you feel _____ about yourself	1. The girl feels **embarrassed** and wants to _____ (base verb) 2. I feel **embarrassed** when I _____ (present-tense verb . . .)
4 **respect** re • **spect** *verb* _____	to feel that someone or something is _____	1. The students **respect** their teacher, so they _____ (present-tense verb . . .) 2. I respect people who are _____ (adjective)

Vocabulary Q&A

 USE NEW WORDS
Discuss the question with your partner.
Then select your favorite idea to write
a complete sentence.

Language to COMPARE

My idea is like yours.
My idea is like (Name)'s.

🎯 Grammar Target

A **present-tense verb** tells what is happening right now or all the time.
Regular **present-tense verbs** change depending on the **subject**.

| *I **eat** pizza.*
*You **eat** pizza.* | *He/She/It **eats** pizza.*
*Leo **eats** pizza.*
*My friend **eats** pizza.* | *We **eat** pizza.*
*They **eat** pizza.* |

1. Question: What do you do in your **culture**?

Frame: In my **culture**, we _____ (**present-tense verb:** *cook . . .*)
and _____ (**present-tense verb:** *celebrate . . .*).

Verbs (action words)					
cook	share	speak	help	celebrate	give
make	visit	drink	eat	dance	like

Answer: _____

_____

2. Question: Who is someone you **respect**?

Frame: One person I **respect** is my _____ (**noun:** *grandmother*)
because (he/she) _____ (**present-tense verb:** *listens . . .*).

Nouns (people)			Verbs (action words)		
friend	teacher	father	supports	knows	helps
mother	grandmother	cousin	listens	talks	acts
grandfather	classmate	brother	makes	loves	understands

Answer: _____

_____

3. Question: How can others **affect** how you feel?

Frame: Others **affect** how I feel when they _____ (**present-tense verb:** *laugh . . .*).

Verbs (action words)			
act	say	give	play
talk	compliment	support	write
help	listen	learn	encourage

Answer: _____

_____

⊙ Grammar Target

The words *a* and *an* come before **singular nouns** and **adjectives** that describe them.

Use *a* if the noun or adjective begins with a **consonant:**	Use *an* if the noun or adjective begins with a **vowel** (*a, e, i, o, u*):
She plays **a** <u>g</u>ame. I see **a** <u>b</u>lack dog.	He eats **an** <u>a</u>pple. It was **an** <u>e</u>asy test.

4. Question: What is an important part of your **identity**?

Frame: An important part of my **identity** is that I am (a/an)
_____ (**adjective:** *caring*) _____ (**noun:** *sister*).

Adjectives (describing words)		Nouns (people)	
helpful	*help other people*	student	sibling
generous	*share things with others*	friend	leader
talented	*good at something*	artist	seamstress
loyal	*always support someone*	grandchild	daughter/son
respectful	*respect others*	athlete	cousin
intelligent	*smart*	dancer	volunteer

Answer: _____

_____

Picture Observations

MAKE OBSERVATIONS

Discuss what you observe about the picture using *is* or *are* and verb + *–ing*.

Grammar Target

Use *is* or *are* and **verb + –ing** to tell about an ongoing action that is happening now.

Singular: *is* and **verb + –ing** *The girl **is wearing** red sneakers.*	**Plural:** *are* and **verb + –ing** *The students **are sitting** down.*

Verbs (action words)			Nouns (people, places, things)		
speaking	showing	talking	outside	tennis racket	hijab
wearing	holding	laughing	students	sneakers	glasses
looking	smiling	sitting	phone	backpack	park

WRITE OBSERVATIONS

Look at the picture. What do you observe about the students?

1. The students _____

2. One girl _____

3. Two girls _____

4. One boy _____

5. Two boys _____

What do you notice in the picture?	I notice that there (is/are) _____.
What else do you notice?	I also notice that _____.
Do you notice anything else?	It looks like _____.

MAKE OBSERVATIONS

Discuss what you observe about the people, place, and things in the picture.

Nouns (people, places, things)

chair
library
bookcase
name tag
school
meeting
group
conversation

WRITE OBSERVATIONS

Look at the picture. Respond to the questions using complete sentences.

1. Where are the students?

The students are in _____

I notice that _____

2. What do you think the girl is doing?

It looks like the girl _____

I notice that she _____

3. What are the other people doing?

I notice that they _____

I also notice that they _____

What's in a Name?

by Manuela Gutierrez

How does your name affect your identity?

What do you know about your name? Your name is an important part of your **identity**. It can tell others about who you are and where you come from. How people **pronounce** your name can also **affect** how you feel. Let's read about where names come from and why they are important.

① NAME ORIGINS
Where do names come from?

Do you know how you got your name? Maybe your parents liked the way it sounded. Or maybe your **culture** has **traditions** about names. For example, some **cultures** in Ghana name children based on the day they were born. A boy born on Thursday might be named Yaw. A girl born on Thursday might be named Yaa. In many Latin **cultures**, the **tradition** is for people to have two last names. One Inuit **tradition** is to name children after older family members.

Some names have meanings in certain languages. The name Farah means happiness in Arabic.

Famous boxer Muhammad Ali was born as Cassius Clay, Jr. He changed his name when he converted to Islam.

Parents might also select a name because of what it means. For example, the name Hu means tiger in Chinese, and Reina means queen in Spanish. In addition, some names honor the **legacies** of people. For example, Muhammad and Sarah are the names of people in religious texts. Many names also honor famous people, like leaders, athletes, or musicians. Names can also honor family members, such as grandparents, aunts, or uncles.

Sometimes, your name's origin or meaning can **affect** your **identity**. If your name means tiger, you might feel big and powerful. If you are named after someone special, you might feel like a part of their **legacy**. The story of your name can be an important part of who you are.

❷ SAY MY NAME
How do you feel when someone mispronounces your name?

Imagine it's your first day at a new school. Your teacher introduces you to the class, but he **pronounces** your name wrong! You are too **embarrassed** to correct him. Now, all of your new classmates think you are someone else!

Mispronouncing someone's name might cause them to feel **embarrassed**.

So, what happens when someone **mispronounces** your name? It can **affect** how you feel about yourself and your **culture**. You might feel **embarrassed** or like you don't belong. For this reason, some people change their name so that it is easier to **pronounce**. Ha-Yun, a ninth-grader from New York, explains, "I like my Korean name, but it's hard for my teachers to say. I tell them to just use my American name, Lucy." Some people might also use their last name or a nickname. Reyansh Razva, a seventh-grader from India, says, "Everyone calls me Razva or Rey instead of my full first name." Others might **pronounce** their name differently in English. For example, a boy named Julián (*Who-lee-AHN*) might go by Julian (*Jool-yen*) in English.

But some people think others should not have to change their names to feel **respected**. For example, there are teachers who are part of a project called "My Name, My Identity." They teach people why it is important to **pronounce** students' names correctly. They want all students to feel welcome and valued at school. Students learn better when they feel like they belong. When you **pronounce** someone's name correctly, you show them that you **respect** them.

Students feel valued at school when classmates **pronounce** their names correctly.

Names can have unique meanings, tell stories, or honor people's **legacies**. The way people **pronounce** our names can also **affect** how we feel. What do you think? How do you feel about your name?

Close Reading

RESPOND TO SECTION 1

Reread Section 1 with a partner. Then answer the questions.

1. What is the main idea of this section?

   A. Names affect your identity.

   B. Some names come from different languages.

   C. Names have many different origins.

   D. Names can come from cultures and traditions.

2. What are two key details in this section?

   A. Hu means tiger in Chinese.

   B. Names can have special meanings.

   C. Sarah is a name in religious texts.

   D. Some names honor the legacies of important people.

RESPOND WITH EVIDENCE

Use the frames to write a response. Include text evidence and precise words.

🎯 Grammar Target

A **plural noun** is a word for more than one person, place, or thing. Add **–s** or **–es** to make a noun plural.

book → books   *lunch → lunches*

Language to COLLABORATE

What could we write?

We could write _____.

Okay. Let's write _____.

Nouns (people, things)		Adjectives (describing words)		Verbs (action words)	
relatives	traditions	famous	popular	mean	come from
leaders	religions	respected	celebrated	honor	respect

What are some ways that people get their names?

Names can come from _____
(plural noun: *cultures*)

Some parents might name their children after _____
(plural noun: *musicians*)

Some people are named after _____ people.
(adjective: *important*)

Some parents choose names that _____
(present-tense verb: *come from . . .*)

RESPOND TO SECTION 2

Reread Section 2 with a partner. Then answer the questions.

1. What is the main idea of this section?

    A. Some people change their names.

    B. It is okay to mispronounce someone's name.

    C. It is difficult to pronounce names in other languages.

    D. The way someone pronounces your name can affect how you feel.

2. What are two key details in this section?

    A. People can feel embarrassed when others mispronounce their name.

    B. A boy named Julián might go by Julian.

    C. Ha-Yun is a ninth-grader from New York.

    D. People feel respected when others pronounce their names correctly.

RESPOND WITH EVIDENCE

Use the frames to write a response. Include text evidence and precise words.

Grammar Target	Language to COLLABORATE
A **base verb** is an action word with no endings. **Base verbs** come after words like *to* and *might*. *I want to **go** home.*　　*I might **feel** happy.*	What could we write? We could write _____. Okay. Let's write _____.

Verbs (action words)		Adjectives (describing words)		Nouns (people, things)	
cause	make	valued	embarrassed	teachers	nickname
affect	disrespect	respected	special	classmates	last name

How can name pronunciation affect people's feelings?

When other people mispronounce your name, it can _____

                                                    (base verb: *affect . . .*)

Students feel _____ when their _____ know how to

               (adjective: *excited*)   (plural noun: *coaches*)

pronounce their names.

Some people might go by (a/their) _____ instead of their first name.

                                         (noun: *last name*)

Academic Discussion

Prompt | How does the pronunciation of your name affect your identity?

BRAINSTORM IDEAS

Work with a partner to write at least three ideas in each column.

Grammar Target

The prefixes *un–* and *dis–* at the beginning of a word mean **not**.

*un*happy → **not** happy *dis*liked → **not** liked

*un*true → **not** true *dis*honest → **not** honest

Positive Adjectives ⊕	Negative Adjectives ⊖
When people **pronounce your name correctly**, you might feel _____.	When people **mispronounce your name,** you might feel _____.
• glad	• _____
• _____	• embarrassed
• excited	• _____
• valued	• unvalued
• important	• un_____
• comfortable	• un_____
• _____	• disrespected
• encouraged	• discouraged

IDENTIFY STRONG WORDS

Review the text and lesson activities. Create a list of strong words about the topic.

	Nouns (people, places, things)	Verbs (action words)	Adjectives (describing words)
Text	• _____ • _____	• _____ • _____	• _____ • _____
Activities	• _____ • _____	• _____ • _____	• _____ • _____

EXPRESS YOUR OPINION
Rewrite two ideas using the frames.
Include strong word choices from
the word bank.

Language to AGREE / DISAGREE

I agree with (Name) because _____.

I disagree with (Name) because _____.

Prompt | How does the pronunciation of your name affect your identity?

Response 1

When people **pronounce your name correctly**, you might feel <u>proud</u> or <u>valued</u>. This **positively** affects your identity because it can cause you to <u>feel connected to your culture</u>.

Response 2

When people **mispronounce your name**, you might feel <u>uncomfortable</u> or <u>upset</u>. This **negatively** affects your identity because it can cause you to <u>want to change your name</u>.

Response 1

When people **pronounce your name correctly**, you might feel _____
(adjective: proud)

or _____ This **positively** affects your identity because it can cause
(adjective: valued)

you to _____
(base verb: remember . . .)

_____

Response 2

When people **mispronounce your name**, you might feel _____
(adjective: unwelcome)

or _____ This **negatively** affects your identity because it can
(adjective: disrespected)

cause you to _____
(base verb: want . . .)

_____

Ten-Minute Response

Prompt	What are the reasons it is important to pronounce names correctly?

Verbs (action words)		Adjectives (describing words)	
honor	to respect	appreciated	valued
demonstrate	to show	welcome	feel like you belong
communicate	to give information	worthy	valued and important
care about	to be interested in	included	part of a group
express	to tell	accepted	belonging to a group
hope	to want	comfortable	relaxed and happy
value	to think something is important	important	having meaning or value

It is important to pronounce names correctly for many reasons. One reason is that it can make people feel <u>welcome</u>. For example, when you pronounce someone's name right, you <u>demonstrate that you appreciate them.</u>

- -

It is important to pronounce names correctly for many reasons. One reason is that it can <u>honor a family member's legacy</u>. For example, when you pronounce someone's name precisely, you show the person that you <u>respect the memory of their relative</u>.

✏️ WRITE TOGETHER
Work with your teacher to write a ten-minute response. Include strong word choices.

It is important to pronounce names correctly for many reasons. One reason

is that it can make people feel <u>respected.</u> For example, when you pronounce
(adjective: *welcome*)

someone's name right, you _____
(present-tense verb: *help . . .*)

_____

_____

✏️ **WRITE WITH A PARTNER**

Work with a partner to write ten-minute responses. Include strong word choices.

> It is important to pronounce names correctly for many reasons. One reason
>
> is that it can make people feel _____ For example, when
> (adjective: *excited*)
>
> you pronounce someone's name right, you _____
> (present-tense verb: *make . . .*)
>
> _____
>
> _____

> It is important to pronounce names correctly for many reasons. One reason is
>
> that it can _____
> (base verb: *show . . .*)
>
> For example, when you pronounce someone's name precisely, you show the
>
> person that you _____
> (present-tense verb: *think . . .*)
>
> _____

✏️ **WRITE ON YOUR OWN**

Write a ten-minute response on your own. Include strong word choices.

> It is important to pronounce names correctly for many reasons. One reason is
>
> that it can _____
> (base verb: *show . . .*)
>
> _____
>
> For example, when you pronounce someone's name precisely, you show the
>
> person that you _____
> (present-tense verb: *want . . .*)
>
> _____

Listen Up!

LISTEN AND RESPOND
Listen to the conversation and take notes.
Then answer the questions.

Language to COMPARE
My question is like yours.
My question is like (Name)'s.

Who is speaking?	What are they talking about?

1. What problem does Bob have?

A. He knows the girl's name.

B. He wants to ask the girl how she is doing.

C. He does not remember the girl's name.

2. One question I have for Shalini is: _____

_____

Listen to the podcast and take notes. Then answer the questions.

Who is speaking?	What are they talking about?

1. Why does Ruby have a lot of names?

A. His culture has a tradition about names.

B. Many people gave him names.

C. His cousin wanted him to have a lot of names.

2. How does Ruby feel about his name?

A. He likes his name.

B. He feels proud of his name.

C. He feels stuck with his name.

3. One question I have for Ruby is: _____

_____

Speak Your Mind

WRITE RESPONSES

What would you say in these situations? Provide strong reasons for your responses.

1. Your teacher mispronounces your name in front of the class.
What would you say to your teacher?

Frame: I would (tell/ask) my teacher _____. One reason is because _____.

_____

_____

2. Your classmate calls you by a nickname, and you don't like it.
What would you say to your classmate?

Frame: I would (tell/ask) my classmate _____. One reason is because _____.

_____

_____

3. Your friends want you to change your name so that it is easier to pronounce.
What would you tell your friends?

Frame: I would (tell/ask) my friends _____. One reason is because _____.

_____

_____

Using Clear Pronunciation

When you share your ideas, use clear pronunciation. Make sure that you:

- pronounce words correctly
- emphasize the right syllables
- do not mumble

Practice clear pronunciation:

When **class**mates mispro**nounce** my name, I cor**rect** them po**lite**ly.

PRESENT IDEAS

Take turns rehearsing each situation with your partner. Restate your partner's response to show you are listening actively and carefully.

Language to RESTATE

So you would (tell/ask) _____?

Yes, that's right.

No, I would (tell/ask) _____.

Past-Tense Verbs

Using Past-Tense Verbs

Writers use **past-tense verbs** to tell about events that happened in the past.

Make the past tense of **regular verbs** by adding an **–ed** ending.
For verbs that end in e, add **–d**.

play → play**ed**	talk → talk**ed**	like → lik**ed**	love → lov**ed**

For **irregular verbs**, you need to memorize the past-tense form.

is → was	give → gave	think → thought	say → said
are → were	know → knew	feel → felt	teach → taught

🔍 IDENTIFY PAST-TENSE VERBS

Change the regular and irregular verbs to their past tense.

Regular Verbs	Irregular Verbs
• want → _____	• give → _____
• honor → _____	• is → _____
• show → _____	• feel → _____
• pronounce → _____	• know → _____

✏️ WRITE PAST-TENSE VERBS

Complete each sentence with the correct past-tense verb from the table above.

Language to COMPARE and CONTRAST

My answer is like (yours/<u>Name</u>'s).

My answer is different from (yours/<u>Name</u>'s).

1. My parents _____ to name me after someone famous.

2. On my first day of school, my teacher _____ my name correctly.

3. Alejandro's new classmates _____ him the nickname "Ale."

4. Rejah _____ embarrassed when the teacher said her name wrong.

5. Ayanna _____ named after her mother.

6. My parents _____ my aunt's legacy by naming me after her.

Sentence Fix-Ups

Today is Ayah's first day of school. She is say hello to the class. The teacher introduces her and pronounce her name correctly. Ayah feels welcomed.

EXPAND AND EDIT

The sentences below have an error. Correct the sentences and rewrite them.

1. She is say hello to the class.

_____

2. The teacher introduces her and pronounce her name correctly.

_____

_____

Rewrite the sentences with more details.

3. Today is Ayah's first day of school.

_____

_____

4. Ayah feels welcomed.

_____

_____

Look at the picture. Write a sentence about what will happen next.

5. _____

_____

Student Writing Models

What is a Narrative?

A **narrative** tells a story about a person's experience.

A The **beginning** introduces the characters and the topic.

B The **middle** gives details about the events in the order that they happened.

C The **end** summarizes the important ideas.

MARK THE PARAGRAPHS

Read each paragraph with a partner. Notice the beginning, middle, and end.

- Circle five past-tense verbs.
- Underline three detail sentences.
- Star four strong word choices.

Language to REACT

I appreciated that the writer _____.

I was surprised that _____.

I enjoyed the writer's _____.

PROMPT 1

My Journey with My Name
by Amna Karame

A I was born 15 years ago, and my parents named me Amna. My family is from Yemen, where

B people speak Arabic. In Arabic, my name means peace. My parents believed that I would bring peace to their lives. At first, I did not like my name. It sounded different from other names in the United States. However, as I got older, I learned to love it. Now, I think my name sounds beautiful. It is an important part of my identity. Even though I did not like my name at first, now I would

C never change it. My name honors my background, my language, and my culture.

PROMPT 2

My New School
by Li Wei Xiang

A Two years ago, I moved to a new school. My parents are from China, so my name is Chinese.

B Some people at my new school thought my name was too difficult to say. On my first day, my teacher told me he would call me Jake. At first, I enjoyed my name change. But a few months later, it started to affect me. It felt like my identity was being erased. Finally, I decided to tell people, "My name is not Jake. It's Li Wei." I explained how to pronounce my name every time someone

C had trouble. Now, people call me by my true name. I finally feel respected at school.

Organize a Narrative

1. Write the story of your name or nickname. Include where it came from or how you got it.
2. Write about a positive or negative experience you had with your name.

 BRAINSTORM IDEAS

Choose one prompt. Use the organizer to plan your paragraph.

What part of your name are you going to write about?

☑ First name: Amna   ❑ Last name(s): _____

❑ Middle name: _____   ❑ Nickname(s): _____

How will your narrative begin? I will write about (how/why/when) . . .

I will write about why my parents chose my name. I will write about what my name means.

What details will you include? I will include details about (how/why/when) . . .

I will include details about how I felt about my name. At first, I did not like it. I will then write about how now I like my name.

How will your narrative end? I will end my narrative with (how/why/when) . . .

I will end my narrative with how I feel the story of my name is special and honors my culture.

What part of your name are you going to write about?

❑ First name: _____   ❑ Last name(s): _____

❑ Middle name: _____   ❑ Nickname(s): _____

How will your narrative begin? I will write about (how/why/when) . . .

What details will you include? I will include details about (how/why/when) . . .

How will your narrative end? I will end my narrative with (how/why/when) . . .

Narrative Writing

✏️ **WRITE TOGETHER**
Write narrative paragraphs using the frames below.

PROMPT 1

My Name and My Culture

I was born _____ years ago in _____ My family
           (number)   (country)

has _____ people and our home language is _____
     (number)   (language)

My name is _____ My family gave me this name because
          (name)

they _____
   (past-tense verb: *thought . . .*)

When I was younger, I _____ my name because I thought it
                  (liked/did not like)

was _____ Now, I think that my name
   (adjective: *easy to say*)

is _____ My name honors my _____
  (adjective: *special*)   (noun: *culture . . .*)

_____

PROMPT 2

My First Day of School

In _____ I came to a new school. At first, I felt _____
  (year)   (adjective: *concerned*)

because I thought my classmates and teacher would think my name sounded

_____ However, my teacher worked hard to pronounce
(adjective: *different*)

my name correctly. Then she _____ the class to pronounce
              (past-tense verb: *helped*)

my name the right way, too. I explained what my name means in my language,

_____ My _____ teacher
(language)   (adjective: *caring*)

helped me feel _____ on my first day. Even though I was
          (adjective: *respected*)

_____ at first, I felt _____ at my new school.
(adjective: *afraid*)   (adjective: *welcome*)

1. Write the story of your name or nickname. Include where it came from or how you got it.
2. Write about a positive or negative experience you had with your name.

✏ WRITE ON YOUR OWN

Write a narrative paragraph with a beginning, middle, and end. Include details, past-tense verbs, and strong word choices. Check your grammar and spelling.

Language to REACT

I enjoyed the interesting _____.

I was surprised that _____.

I appreciated how you _____.

Title: _____

Author: _____

_____

_____

_____

_____

_____

_____

_____

_____

_____

_____

_____

KEEPING LANGUAGES ALIVE

Activate Knowledge

💡 BRAINSTORM IDEAS

Brainstorm precise words to complete the frame.

Question: How do you communicate with your family and friends?

Frame: I communicate with my (family/friends) by _____ (**verb + –ing**: *writing . . .*).

▶ I communicate with my <u>family</u> by <u>speaking Chinese with my parents</u>.

▶ I communicate with my <u>friends</u> by <u>sending messages on social media</u>.

> **🎯 Grammar Target**
>
> After *by*, use **verb + –ing** to give more information about an action that happens often.
>
> *He travels <u>by</u> **taking the bus.***
>
> *I relax <u>by</u> **reading a book.***

Verbs (action words)			Nouns (people, places, things)		
speaking	writing	chatting	text messages	English	emails
calling	sending	creating	videos	phone	video chat

I communicate with my family by _____ (verb + –ing . . .).	I communicate with my friends by _____ (verb + –ing . . .).
• _____ • _____ • _____	• _____ • _____ • _____

✏️ WRITE IDEAS

Select your two favorite ideas and write complete sentences.

> **Language to COMPARE**
>
> My idea is the same as yours.
>
> My idea is the same as (<u>Name</u>)'s.

1. _____

_____

2. _____

_____

Academic Vocabulary

BUILD WORD KNOWLEDGE
Complete the meanings and examples for the academic words.

Language to SHARE IDEAS

Which idea did you select?
I selected _____.

Word	Meaning	Picture and Examples
1 **generation** gen • er • a • tion *noun* _____ _____	a group of people who are about the same _____ 🌐	1. Your _____ (plural noun) are relatives from an older **generation**. 2. Younger **generations** might know more about _____ (plural noun) than older **generations**.
2 **benefit** ben • e • fit *noun* _____ _____	something that is _____ for you or helps you 🌐	1. A **benefit** of eating healthy food is that it can help people _____ (present-tense verb . . .) 2. A **benefit** of practicing English is that you _____ (present-tense verb . . .)
3 **challenge** chal • lenge *noun* _____ _____	something that is _____ 🌐	1. For some people, it is a **challenge** to _____ (base verb . . .) _____ 2. It can be a **challenge** for students to get to school on time if they _____ (present-tense verb . . .)
4 **connected** con • nec • ted *adjective* _____	feel _____ to someone or something 🌐	1. When classmates _____ (present-tense verb) each other every day, they feel **connected**. 2. I feel **connected** to my friends when I _____ (present-tense verb . . .)

Activate Knowledge

Grammar Target

Adverbs describe actions.
Adverbs of frequency describe how often an action happens.

never: no times	0%
sometimes: a few times	25%
often: many times	75%
always: all the time	100%

BRAINSTORM IDEAS

Brainstorm precise words to complete the frame.

Question: When do you speak your native language?

Frame: I _____ (**adverb**: *often*) speak my native language when I _____ (**present-tense verb**: *buy* . . .).

▶ I never speak my native language when I talk to the principal at my school.

▶ I sometimes speak my native language when I play baseball at the park.

▶ I often speak my native language when I hang out with my cousin.

▶ I always speak my native language when I call my aunt in Beijing.

Verbs (action words)				
go to	participate	talk to	chat with	coach
play	volunteer	discuss	hang out	buy

	speak my native language when I _____ (present-tense verb . . .).
I never . . .	• _____
I sometimes . . .	• _____
I often . . .	• _____
I always . . .	• _____

WRITE IDEAS

Select your two favorite ideas and write complete sentences.

Language to COMPARE

My idea is the same as yours.

My idea is the same as (Name)'s.

1. _____

_____

2. _____

_____

Academic Vocabulary

BUILD WORD KNOWLEDGE

Complete the meanings and examples for the academic words.

Language to SHARE IDEAS

Which idea did you select?

I selected _____.

Word	Meaning	Picture and Examples
1 **essential** es • **sen** • tial *adjective* _____ _____	very _____ _____ 🌐 _____	1. Many people think it is **essential** to _____ (base verb . . .) _____ 2. At school, it is **essential** to _____ (base verb . . .) _____ if you want to learn new things.
2 **communicate** com • **mu** • ni • cate *verb* _____ _____	to share information or _____ with other people 🌐 _____	1. With a phone, people can _____ (base verb) to **communicate**. 2. The language I prefer to **communicate** in is _____ (language)
3 **dominant** dom • i • nant *adjective* _____ _____	most _____ _____ 🌐 _____	1. The **dominant** weather in the summer is _____ (adjective) 2. I practice speaking my **dominant** language with my _____ (noun)
4 **encourage** en • **cour** • age *verb* _____ _____	to _____ or suggest that someone do something 🌐 _____	1. Parents can **encourage** their children to _____ (base verb . . .) 2. Many teachers **encourage** their students to _____ (base verb . . .)

Vocabulary Q&A

 USE NEW WORDS
Discuss the question with your partner.
Then select your favorite idea to write
a complete sentence.

Language to COMPARE

My idea is the same as yours.

My idea is the same as (Name)'s.

1. Question: What are two **benefits** of going to school?

Frame: Two **benefits** of going to school are that I can _____ (**base verb:** *learn . . .*)
and _____ (**base verb:** *see . . .*).

Verbs (action words)			Nouns (people, places, things)		
read	improve	participate in	friends	topics	stories
write	practice	connect with	English	vocabulary	subjects
speak	meet	understand	words	ideas	books

Answer: _____

_____

Grammar Target

After *with*, use **verb + –ing** to give more information about an action that happens
regularly or often.

I struggle <u>*with*</u> **cleaning my room**.   *I have trouble* <u>*with*</u> **waking up early**.

2. Question: What are two **challenges** you have at school?

Frame: Two **challenges** I have at school are with _____ (**verb + –ing:** *studying . . .*)
and _____ (**verb + –ing:** *writing . . .*).

Verbs (action words)			Nouns (people, places, things)		
learning	meeting	remembering	math	books	science
speaking	understanding	making	friends	essays	projects
reading	completing	creating	English	assignments	new ideas

Answer: _____

_____

3. Question: How do you feel **connected** to other people?

Frame: I feel **connected** to other people when
    they _____ (**present-tense verb:** *encourage* . . .).

Verbs (action words)			
act	participate	provide	play
share	compliment	support	write
help	listen	learn	encourage

Answer: _____

_____

🎯 Grammar Target

Don't forget! After <u>by</u>, use **verb + –ing** to give more information about an action that happens often.

*Alan talks to his dad <u>by</u> **calling him every day**.*	*I share photos <u>by</u> **texting them to my friends**.*

4. Question: How do you **communicate** with people?

Frame: I **communicate** with my _____ (**plural noun:** *cousins*)
    by _____ (**verb + –ing:** *speaking* . . .).

Nouns (people)		Verbs (action words)		
parents	teachers	sending	sharing	using
classmates	family members	creating	writing	drawing
siblings	grandparents	posting	emailing	video chatting

Answer: _____

_____

Picture Observations

 MAKE OBSERVATIONS

Discuss what you observe about the picture using *is* or *are* and verb + *–ing*.

Verbs (action words)	
holding	posing
wearing	taking
sitting	standing
smiling	leaning
carrying	looking

Nouns (people, places, things)	
flag	phone
picture	stroller
outside	sidewalk
hijabs	sunglasses
purse	city

Grammar Target

Don't forget! Use *is* or *are* and **verb + –ing** to tell about an ongoing action that is happening now.

Singular: *is* and **verb + –ing**	**Plural:** *are* and **verb + –ing**
One woman *is wearing* a hat.	The women *are wearing* sunglasses.

WRITE OBSERVATIONS

Look at the picture. Write your observations about the people in the picture.

1. The women _____

2. Two women _____

3. Most of the women _____

4. All women except for the little girl _____

5. The little girl _____

What do you notice in the picture?	I notice that there (is/are) _____.
What else do you notice?	I also notice that _____.
Do you notice anything else?	It looks like _____.

MAKE OBSERVATIONS

Discuss what you observe about the people, place, and things in the picture.

Nouns (people, places, things)	
parade	outfit
dragon	city

Verbs (action words)	
celebrating	carrying
participating	running

Adjectives (describing words)	
traditional	busy
colorful	many

WRITE OBSERVATIONS

Look at the picture. Respond to the questions using complete sentences.

Grammar Target

Prepositions can tell the location of a noun.

*The dancers are **outside**. The parade is **in** the city.*

1. Where are the people?

The people are _____

I notice that they are _____

2. What do you think the people are doing?

It looks like the people _____

I notice that they _____

I also notice that they _____

Watch Your Language!

by Baba Galleh

How do languages stay alive?

Did you know there are more than 7,000 languages in the world? However, 3,000 of these languages are in danger. Soon they might not have any speakers left. The best way to preserve, or protect, a language is by speaking it. Then, you can pass it down to the next **generation**. But this is not always easy! Let's read about the **benefits** and **challenges** of continuing to speak your native language.

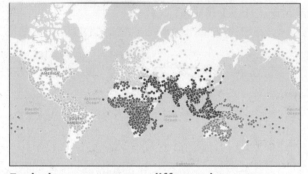

Languages of the World

Each dot represents a different language spoken in each region. Asia and Africa have the most languages.

❶ BENEFITS

What are the benefits of continuing to speak your native language?

There are many **benefits** of continuing to speak your native language. First, your native language is one way to stay **connected** to your family's history and culture. "Speaking Arabic is an **essential** part of who I am," says Nizar Karamé, a 16-year-old originally from Lebanon. "I speak it at all my family gatherings and celebrations." Second, there are many **benefits** to your brain when you regularly speak another language. For instance, studies show that speaking two languages can improve your memory. It can also make your brain healthier.

Many Chinese-speakers outside of China still celebrate Chinese New Year, an important cultural tradition.

In addition, knowing your native language can help you **communicate** with older **generations** or relatives in other countries. For example, you can call them or send them messages. You feel **connected** to others when it is easy to **communicate** with them. Finally, if you speak your native language, you can pass it down to the next **generation**. This helps keep your native language alive.

CHALLENGES

What are the challenges of continuing to speak your native language?

New **generations** born in the United States often learn English very early in school.

When you live in a country where English is **dominant**, it can be a **challenge** to continue speaking a **non-dominant** language. For example, Ganak Ramjah, a 15-year-old from Houston, explains, "My parents are from India. They **encourage** me to speak Hindi, but it is easier to speak English. Everybody speaks English here. Only my family speaks Hindi." In addition, future **generations** born in English-speaking countries often learn English at a young age. As a result, English might become their **dominant** language. If it is easier to **communicate** in English, you might feel **disconnected** from your family's language or think it is not **essential** to your life.

Another **challenge** is that there might not be enough people in your life who speak your native language. For example, some people only speak their native language at home or with relatives in another country. If you do not regularly practice your native language, it might become more difficult to speak it. Finally, some families **encourage** their children to speak only English. They think this will help them be successful in a country where English is **dominant**.

Some families **encourage** their children to speak only English.

There can be many **benefits** to continuing to speak your native language. However, there are also many **challenges**. How do you feel about speaking your native language? Do you think it is **essential** to preserve your language for future **generations**?

Close Reading

RESPOND TO SECTION 1

Reread Section 1 with a partner. Then answer the questions.

1. What is the main idea of this section?

    A. When you can communicate with someone, you feel close to them.

    B. Language is important to your identity.

    C. There are many benefits to speaking a language that is not dominant.

    D. Some people speak to their grandparents in different languages.

2. What are two key details in this section?

    A. Passing a language down to future generations is the only way to protect it.

    B. Your brain is healthier when you speak more than one language.

    C. Your native language can help you feel connected to your family and culture.

    D. Great-grandparents are family members from older generations.

RESPOND WITH EVIDENCE

Use the frames to write a response. Include text evidence and precise words.

◎ Grammar Target
A **plural noun** is a word for more than one person, place, or thing. Some plural nouns are irregular. For example, *child → children*.

Language to COLLABORATE
What could we write?
We could write _____.
Okay. Let's write _____.

Nouns (people, things)			Verbs (action words)	
history	identity	children	call	email
culture	traditions	memory	text	communicate with

What are the benefits of continuing to speak your native language?

You can stay connected to your family's _____

(noun: *culture*)

You can improve your _____

(noun: *memory*)

People can pass down their native language to their _____

(noun: *nieces*)

You can _____ family members from older generations.

(base verb: *speak* . . .)

RESPOND TO SECTION 2

Reread Section 2 with a partner. Then answer the questions.

1. What is the main idea of this section?

  A. Some families choose not to use their native language.

  B. There are many challenges with continuing to speak your native language.

  C. Some languages are non-dominant languages.

  D. Some communities might not speak your family's language.

2. What are two key details in this section?

  A. There might not be enough people in your life to practice your language with.

  B. All children in the United States learn English in school.

  C. Sometimes it is easier to speak a country's dominant language.

  D. Older generations might not feel connected to their family's language.

RESPOND WITH EVIDENCE

Use the frames to write a response. Include text evidence and precise words.

⊚ Grammar Target	Language to COLLABORATE
Don't forget! A **base verb** is an action word with no endings. **Base verbs** often come after words like *to* and *might*.	What could we write? We could write _____. Okay. Let's write _____.

Adjectives (describing words)			Verbs (action words)	
common	necessary	important	encourage	speak
dominant	useful	essential	want	practice

What are the challenges of continuing to speak your native language?

Sometimes, it is easier to speak the _____ language.
(adjective: *common*)

There might not be enough people in your life to _____ your
native language with.　(base verb: *practice*)

New generations might feel like their native language is not _____
(adjective: *essential*)

Some families might _____ their children to speak English.
(base verb: *prefer*)

Academic Discussion

Prompt	What are the benefits and challenges of continuing to speak your native language?

BRAINSTORM IDEAS

Work with a partner to write three ideas in each column.

Grammar Target

Some **verbs** act like **adjectives** when they end in *–ed* or *–d*.	*connected* → feel close to someone or something *encouraged* → feel supported to do something

Benefits ⊕	Challenges ⊖
One important **benefit** of continuing to speak your native language is that you can _____. • stay connected to your family and culture • communicate with _____ _____ • pass it down to _____ _____ • help to preserve _____ _____	One **challenge** of continuing to speak your native language is that you might _____. • think it is easier to speak the dominant language • not have enough _____ to speak it with • feel encouraged to _____ _____ • learn to speak English _____ _____

IDENTIFY STRONG WORDS

Review the text and lesson activities. Create a list of strong words about the topic.

	Nouns (people, places, things)	Verbs (action words)	Adjectives (describing words)
Text	• _____ • _____	• _____ • _____	• _____ • _____
Activities	• _____ • _____	• _____ • _____	• _____ • _____

EXPRESS YOUR OPINION
Rewrite two ideas using the frames.
Include strong word choices from
the word bank.

Language to AGREE / DISAGREE

I agree with (<u>Name</u>) because _____.
I disagree with (<u>Name</u>) because _____.

Prompt	What are the benefits and challenges of continuing to speak your native language?

Response 1

One important **benefit** of continuing to speak your native language is that you can <u>pass it down</u> <u>to future generations</u>. As a result, when you continue to speak your native language, you can <u>help</u> <u>preserve it so that it doesn't disappear</u>.

Response 2

One **challenge** of continuing to speak your native language is that you might <u>think it is easier to</u> <u>speak the dominant language</u>. As a result, you might not <u>speak your native language with your</u> <u>friends and classmates</u>.

Response 1

One important **benefit** of continuing to speak your native language is that you

can _____
　　　(base verb: *talk* . . .)

As a result, when you continue to speak your native language, you can

_____
(base verb: *learn* . . .)

Response 2

One **challenge** of continuing to speak your native language is that you might

_____
(base verb: *have trouble* . . .)

As a result, you might not _____
　　　　　　　　　　　(base verb: *want* . . .)

_____

Ten-Minute Response

Prompt	What are the reasons people continue or stop speaking their native language?

Verbs (action words)		Adjectives (describing words)	
demonstrate	*to show or tell*	connected to	*part of something*
maintain	*to keep*	disconnected	*not connected*
preserve	*to protect*	accepted by	*belong to a group*
value	*to think is important*	unaccepted by	*not belong to a group*
improve	*to make better*	uncomfortable	*not relaxed or happy*
dislike	*to not like*	protective of	*wanting to protect*
communicate	*to share information*	discouraged	*not encouraged*
pass down	*to go from one to another*	proud	*feel good about something you did*

There are many reasons people **continue** speaking their native language. One reason is that people might feel <u>protective of their language</u>. For example, when you continue to speak your native language, you can <u>pass it down to future generations and increase the number of speakers</u>.

- -

There are many reasons people **stop** speaking their native language. One reason is that people might feel <u>discouraged from speaking English</u>. For example, some people might <u>have families who want them to only speak English</u>.

✏️ **WRITE TOGETHER**

Work with your teacher to write a ten-minute response. Include strong word choices.

There are many reasons people **continue** speaking their native language. One

reason is that people might feel <u>proud of their ability to speak another language.</u>
(adjective: *happy about . . .*)

For example, when you continue to speak your native language, you can

_____
(base verb: *practice . . .*)

_____

✏️ WRITE WITH A PARTNER

Work with a partner to write ten-minute responses. Include strong word choices.

There are many reasons people **continue** speaking their native language.

One reason is that people might feel _____
(adjective: *accepted by . . .*)

_____

For example, when you continue to speak your native language, you can

_____
(base verb: *speak . . .*)

_____

There are many reasons people **stop** speaking their native language. One

reason is that people might feel _____
(adjective: *discouraged . . .*)

_____

For example, some people might _____
(base verb: *dislike . . .*)

_____

✏️ WRITE ON YOUR OWN

Write a ten-minute response on your own. Include strong word choices.

There are many reasons people **continue** speaking their native language.

One reason is that people might feel _____
(adjective: *comfortable . . .*)

_____

For example, when you continue to speak your native language, you can

_____
(base verb: *express . . .*)

_____

Listen Up!

LISTEN AND RESPOND
Listen to the conversation and take notes. Then answer the questions.

Who is speaking?	What are they talking about?

1. What is Abu's problem?

   A. He did not do well on his test.

   B. He misses his family.

   C. It is difficult to communicate.

2. How will Ms. Aman help Abu?

   A. She will teach him more English.

   B. She will learn words in his language.

   C. She will not give him any homework.

3. One question I have for Abu is: _____

_____

Listen to the presentation and look at the map. Then write and present a summary.

Languages of the World

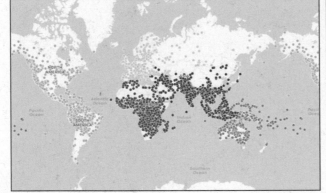

Key Terms	
dominant *(adj)*	*most common*
endangered *(adj)*	*in danger of dying out*
indigenous *(adj)*	*native or tribal*
language *(noun)*	*way of communicating*
maintain *(verb)*	*to keep or preserve*
speaker *(noun)*	*a person who speaks a language*

Summary: The map shows that there are thousands of _____ that

(plural noun)

people speak all over the world. Some languages are _____, and

(adjective)

others are not. For example, _____ languages do not have as many

(adjective)

_____ As a result, these languages are _____

(plural noun)   (adjective)

However, some people are fighting to _____ these languages.

(base verb)

Speak Your Mind

WRITE RESPONSES

Look closely at the map and table. Then use the frames to write responses.

Languages of the World

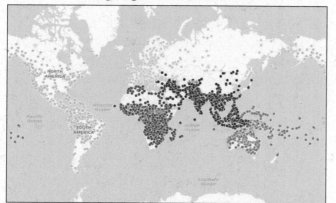

Each dot represents a different language.

Number of Languages by Region	
Africa	2,140
Americas	1,060
Asia	2,300
Pacific	1,310
Europe	290

Table Source: *CIA World Factbook*
Map Source: *Ethnologue: Languages of the World*

1. Summarize what the map and table show in a complete sentence.

   The map and table show _____

   _____

2. Do the map and table support the claim? Use evidence to support your answer.

   Claim: People speak more languages in Europe than in Africa.

   Response: The map and table _____ this claim.
   _(support/do not support)

   One piece of evidence is that the _____ shows that _____
   _(map/table)

   _____

Maintaining Eye Contact

When you present ideas during class, maintain eye contact. Make sure that you:

- look at your partner or classmates often
- look up from your notes every few seconds to engage your listeners

PRESENT IDEAS

Take turns summarizing what the map and table show and stating if they support the claim. Restate your partner's response to show you are listening actively and carefully.

Language to RESTATE

So what you're saying is _____?

Yes, that's right.

No, what I meant was _____.

Modal Verbs

Using Modal Verbs

Writers use **modal verbs** to tell about actions that are **possible** or **need to happen**. Modal verbs <u>never change form</u> and are often followed by a **base verb**.

- Use **can** to tell about **something you believe a person is able to do.**

  *He **can** use his native language to speak with relatives in another country.*

- Use **should** to tell about **something you believe needs to happen now.**

  *People **should** continue to speak their native language.*

- Use **might** to tell about **something you believe is possible when you aren't sure.**

  *Some families **might** want their children to speak English.*

IDENTIFY MODAL VERBS

Read each sentence. Circle the modal verb and underline the base verb.

1. I believe students should learn another language in school.

2. If I practice my English, I know I can speak better.

3. Pablo's classmates might want to help him with his project.

4. Selma can learn more Arabic if she practices every day.

WRITE MODAL VERBS

Complete each sentence with the correct modal verb.

Language to COMPARE and CONTRAST

My answer is the same as (yours/<u>Name</u>'s).

My answer is different from (yours/<u>Name</u>'s).

1. Arami _____ want to talk to her friends in English.

2. My sister _____ read difficult books without help.

3. My brother thinks everyone _____ talk to their friends regularly.

4. I _____ try to get to school on time.

5. Gabriel _____ have to watch his sister after school today.

6. My mother thinks I _____ get a haircut this weekend.

Sentence Fix-Ups

Hassan work on a writing assignment for school. His dad is help him. Hassan wants to check his spelling. His dad helps him use a dictionary.

EXPAND AND EDIT

The sentences below have an error. Correct the sentences and rewrite them.

1. Hassan work on a writing assignment for school.

_____

2. His dad is help him.

_____

Combine the two sentences into one sentence.

Grammar Target	
Use a **comma** and the words **and, but**, and **so** to connect ideas.	• *I like to play mahjong,* **and** *I also enjoy reading.* • *I like to play mahjong,* **but** *I enjoy reading more.* • *I like to play mahjong,* **so** *I play every day.*

3. Hassan wants to check his spelling. His dad helps him use a dictionary.

_____

_____

Look at the picture. Write a sentence about what will happen next.

4. _____

_____

Student Writing Models

What is an Opinion Paragraph?
An **opinion paragraph** states and supports a claim with reasons and evidence.

A The **introductory sentence** states the claim.

B **Detail sentences** support the claim with reasons, evidence, and experiences.

C The **concluding sentence** restates the claim.

⊘ MARK THE PARAGRAPHS
Read each paragraph with a partner.

- Put brackets around the claim.
- Circle four modal verbs.
- Underline two reasons.
- Star four strong word choices.

Language to REACT

I appreciated how the writer _____.

I was surprised that _____.

I especially liked how the writer _____.

EXAMPLE 1

Speaking My Family's Language
by El Hossin Abad

A   In my opinion, you should continue to speak your native language after you learn English. One

reason is there are many health benefits. According to the text, you can improve your brain's

B memory. Another reason is speaking your native language can help you stay connected to your

family's culture. For example, my grandparents can tell me about family traditions in Arabic.

C In conclusion, there are many significant benefits to continuing to speak your native language.

EXAMPLE 2

Only Speaking English
by Fernanda Ortega

A   In my opinion, you should not continue to speak your native language after you learn English. One

reason is that you might not have people to practice speaking your native language with. According

B to the text, it can be difficult to keep speaking your native language if you don't regularly have the

chance to practice it. Another reason is it can be easier to communicate in English. For example,

I always speak English with my friends and neighbors. In conclusion, there are many significant

C challenges to continuing to speak your native language.

Organize an Opinion Paragraph

Prompt: Should you still speak your native language after you learn English?

BRAINSTORM IDEAS

Use the organizer to plan your opinion paragraph.

What is your claim?
In my opinion, you ___should___ continue to speak your native language after you learn English.   (should/should not)

What reasons and evidence will you include to support your claim?	
One reason is there are many health benefits.	**Another reason is** speaking your native language can help you stay connected to your family's culture.
According to the text, you can improve your brain's memory.	**For example,** my grandparents can tell me about family traditions in Arabic.

What is your concluding sentence?
In conclusion, there are many significant ___benefits___ to continuing to speak your native language.   (benefits/challenges)

What is your claim?
In my opinion, you _____ continue to speak your native   (should/should not)   language after you learn English.

What reasons and evidence will you include to support your claim?	
One reason is	Another reason is
According to the text,	For example,

What is your concluding sentence?
In conclusion, there are many significant _____ to continuing   (benefits/challenges)   to speak your native language.

Opinion Writing

✏️ **WRITE TOGETHER**
Write opinion paragraphs using the frames below.

EXAMPLE 1

My Family's Language

In my opinion, you **should** continue speaking your native language after

you learn English. One reason is that language is (a/an) _____ part
(adjective: *essential*)

of your identity. For example, you can _____ connections to
(base verb: *maintain*)

your family's cultural traditions. Another reason is that you can communicate with

_____ According to the text, _____
(plural noun: *relatives*)   (evidence from text)

_____

_____ In conclusion, there are many significant

_____ to continuing to speak your native language.
(benefits/challenges)

EXAMPLE 2

English Only, Please

In my opinion, you **should not** continue speaking your native language after

you learn English. One reason is that it could be _____ to
(adjective: *comfortable*)

speak the dominant language. For example, you might not _____
(base verb: *understand*)

your family's language as well as you know English. Another reason is that people

might not _____ the non-dominant language where you live.
(base verb: *speak*)

According to the text, _____
(evidence from text)

_____ In conclusion, there are many significant

_____ to continuing to speak your native language.
(benefits/challenges)

Prompt: Should you still speak your native language after you learn English?

WRITE ON YOUR OWN
Write an opinion paragraph. State your claim and give reasons and evidence. Include modal verbs and strong word choices. Check your grammar and spelling.

Language to REACT

I appreciated how you _____.

I was surprised that _____.

I especially liked how you _____.

Title: _____

Author: _____

_____

_____

_____

_____

_____

_____

_____

_____

_____

_____

_____

_____

YOUR BRAIN AND LANGUAGE

Activate Knowledge

💡 **BRAINSTORM IDEAS**
Brainstorm precise words to complete the frame.

Question: What activities do you enjoy doing in your native language?

Frame: (One/Another) activity I enjoy doing in my native language is _____ (**verb + –ing**: *listening . . .*).

Grammar Target

Sometimes, a **verb + –ing** can act as a **noun**. For example:
*One activity I enjoy is **reading**.*
Reading is a thing, an activity.

▶ <u>One</u> activity I enjoy doing in my native language is <u>watching movies</u>.

▶ <u>Another</u> activity I enjoy doing in my native language is <u>calling my uncle</u>.

Verbs (action words)			Nouns (people, places, things)		
understanding	visiting	meeting	music	country	books
experiencing	learning	listening	videos	family	conversations

(One/Another) activity I enjoy doing in my native language is _____ (verb + –ing . . .).	
• _____ • _____ • _____	• _____ • _____ • _____

✏️ **WRITE IDEAS**
Select your two favorite ideas and write complete sentences.

Language to COMPARE

My idea is similar to yours.
My idea is similar to (Name)'s.

1. _____

_____

2. _____

_____

Academic Vocabulary

BUILD WORD KNOWLEDGE
Complete the meanings and examples for the academic words.

Language to SHARE IDEAS

Which idea did you choose?
I chose _____.

Word	Meaning	Picture and Examples
1 **responsible** re • **spon** • si • ble *adjective* _____ _____	having a specific _____ to do	**1.** The father is **responsible** for _____ (verb + –ing . . .) _____ **2.** I am **responsible** for _____ (verb + –ing . . .)
2 **multilingual** mul • ti • **lin** • gual *adjective* _____ _____	able to speak more than one _____ _____	**1.** She is **multilingual**, so she _____ (present-tense verb) many languages. **2.** One benefit of being **multilingual** is that you can _____ (base verb . . .) _____
3 **impact** im • pact *noun* _____ _____	the _____ of one thing on another thing	**1.** Rainy weather can have an **impact** on your _____ (noun) **2.** One **impact** of practicing a hobby often is that you can _____ (base verb . . .) _____
4 **compete** com • **pete** *noun* _____ _____	to try to do _____ than others at something	**1.** The mom and daughter **compete** when they _____ (present-tense verb . . .) _____ **2.** I like to **compete** with my friends by _____ (verb + –ing . . .)

Activate Knowledge

BRAINSTORM IDEAS

Brainstorm precise words to complete the frame.

Question: How do you feel when you speak English?

Frame : When I speak English, I _____ (**adverb:** *often*) feel _____ (**adjective:** *intelligent*).

	Grammar Target

Don't forget! Adverbs of frequency describe how often an action happens.

never: no times		0%
sometimes: a few times		25%
often: many times		75%
always: all the time		100%

▶ When I speak English, I <u>never</u> feel <u>scared</u>.

▶ When I speak English, I <u>sometimes</u> feel <u>frustrated</u>.

▶ When I speak English, I <u>often</u> feel <u>smart</u>.

▶ When I speak English, I <u>always</u> feel <u>excited</u>.

Adjectives (describing words)			
frustrated	*annoyed or upset*	confident	*can do something well*
timid	*shy or afraid*	accomplished	*reached a goal*
challenged	*that something is difficult*	talented	*have a special ability*

When I speak English, I _____ (adverb) . . .	feel _____ (adjective).
• _____	• _____
• _____	• _____
• _____	• _____
• _____	• _____

Language to COMPARE

My idea is similar to yours.

My idea is similar to (Name)'s.

WRITE IDEAS

Select your two favorite ideas and write complete sentences.

1. _____

_____

2. _____

_____

Academic Vocabulary

BUILD WORD KNOWLEDGE

Complete the meanings and examples for the academic words.

Language to SHARE IDEAS

Which idea did you choose?

I chose _____.

Word	Meaning	Picture and Examples
1 **manage** man • age *verb* _____ _____	to have _____ of something 🌐	**1.** Some people **manage** their schedules with a _____ (noun) **2.** When I am sad, I **manage** my feelings by _____ (verb + –ing . . .) _____
2 **flexible** flex • i • ble *adjective* _____ _____	able to _____ or do different things 🌐	**1.** He is **flexible** because he can _____ (base verb . . .) _____ **2.** I am **flexible** when I have to _____ (base verb . . .) _____
3 **community** com • **mu** • ni • ty *noun* _____	a group of _____ who live in the same area 🌐	**1.** People help their **community** when they _____ (present-tense verb . . .) **2.** In my **community**, people often speak _____ (language)
4 **constantly** con • stant • ly *adverb* _____	describes when something _____ happens 🌐	**1.** The teacher **constantly** has to remind the class to _____ (base verb . . .) _____ **2.** At school, I **constantly** have to _____ (base verb . . .)

Vocabulary Q&A

 USE NEW WORDS

Discuss the question with your partner. Then select your favorite idea to write a complete sentence.

Grammar Target

Don't forget! Add –s to a **present-tense verb** when the subject is *he*, *she*, *it*, or a singular noun.

- *I love to play soccer.*
- *My sister helps me practice every day.*
- *She wants me to score more goals.*

1. Question: Who has a positive **impact** on your life?

Frame: My _____ (**noun:** *aunt*) has a positive **impact** on my life because (he/she) _____ (**present-tense verb:** *encourages* . . .).

Nouns (people)			Verbs (action words)		
teammate	neighbor	parent	compliments	supports	believes
leader	counselor	friend	connects with	encourages	enjoys
classmate	teacher	sibling	communicates	understands	laughs

Answer: _____

_____

2. Question: What is something you do **constantly**?

Frame: One thing I do **constantly** is _____ (**present-tense verb:** *watch* . . .).

Verbs (action words)			Nouns (people, places, things)		
play	check	learn	family	clothes	project
encourage	practice	share	computer games	sports	English
look at	talk to	listen to	books	phone	music

Answer: _____

_____

Don't forget! After **prepositions**, such as _for_ or _by_, use **verb + –ing** to give more information about an action that happens regularly.

> _José is responsible_ _for_ **clearing** _the table after dinner_.

> _Ahnjong entertains her sister_ _by_ **reading to her**.

3. Question: What are you **responsible** for at school?

Frame: At school, I am **responsible** for _____ (**verb + –ing**: _paying attention . . ._) and _____ (**verb + –ing**: _contributing . . ._).

Verbs (action words)			
taking care of	_being in charge of_	contributing	_giving_
attending	_being present at_	participating	_being part of something_
assisting	_helping with_	modeling	_being an example_

Answer: _____

_____

4. Question: How do you participate in your **community**?

Frame: I participate in my **community** by _____ (**verb + –ing**: _visiting . . ._).

Verbs (action words)			Nouns (people, places, things)		
cleaning	volunteering	planning	food	events	friends
sharing	assisting	talking to	neighbors	flowers	family members
visiting	calling	bringing	parks	parties	projects

Answer: _____

_____

Picture Observations

MAKE OBSERVATIONS

Discuss what you observe about the picture using *is* or *are* and verb + *–ing*.

Grammar Target

Don't forget! Use *is* or *are* and **verb + *–ing*** to tell about an ongoing action that is happening now.

Singular: *is* and **verb + *–ing***
*The girl **is wearing** a green shirt.*

Plural: *are* and **verb + *–ing***
*The students **are standing** outside.*

Verbs (action words)			Nouns (people, places, things)		
standing	talking	enjoying	locker	arms	school
holding	carrying	smiling	backpacks	notebook	jeans
opening	folding	laughing	conversation	outside	hair

WRITE OBSERVATIONS

Look at the picture. What do you observe about the students?

1. The girls _____

2. One girl _____

3. Two girls _____

4. Two girls _____

5. All three girls _____

Language to OBSERVE

What do you notice in the picture?	I notice that there (is/are) _____.
What else do you notice?	I also notice that _____.
Do you notice anything else?	It looks like _____.

 MAKE OBSERVATIONS

Discuss what you observe about the people, place, and things in the picture.

Verbs (action words)

meeting	enjoying
laughing	working
sharing	discussing

Nouns (people, places, things)

restaurant	students
conversation	afternoon
coffee shop	project

WRITE OBSERVATIONS

Look at the picture. Respond to the questions using complete sentences.

1. Who do you think the people are?

It looks like the people are _____

I notice that they _____

2. Where are the people?

It looks like they are _____

I notice that there _____

3. Why do you think the people are together?

It looks like they _____

I also notice that they _____

Your Brain on Languages

by Jia Huang

How are language and your brain connected?

Did you know your brain only weighs three pounds? That's only one pound more than a pineapple! Your brain might not weigh much, but it is very powerful. Your brain is **responsible** for many things, including language. You need your brain to process, or speak, hear, and understand, language. If you are **multilingual**, your brain changes in interesting ways. Let's learn more about the **impact** that being **multilingual** has on the brain.

We speak with our mouths, but our brains are **responsible** for language.

❶ LANGUAGE IN THE BRAIN
How do languages work inside the brain?

Many years ago, scientists thought the **multilingual** brain had separate parts for each language. They also thought there was a limit to how many languages you could learn. However, we now know this is not true. There is no limit to how many languages you can learn! All languages live in the same places in the brain. As a result, the language parts of your brain grow to make room for new languages. This is one of the many interesting **impacts** that being **multilingual** can have on your brain.

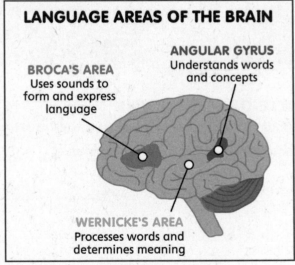

LANGUAGE AREAS OF THE BRAIN

BROCA'S AREA
Uses sounds to form and express language

ANGULAR GYRUS
Understands words and concepts

WERNICKE'S AREA
Processes words and determines meaning

Multilingual brains have to search through multiple languages to find the right words when speaking.

Have you ever tried to say a word in English, but your brain wants you to say it in your native language? There's a reason for this! Since languages live in the same parts of your brain, a new language **competes** with the language already inside your brain. At first, your native language is more dominant. Eventually, your brain learns to **manage** both languages when you speak. Over time, your brain becomes so **flexible** that you don't even realize it is **managing** multiple languages!

❷ SWITCHING LANGUAGES
What are the benefits and challenges of switching between languages?

Students can use their native language to build and grow their new language.

There are many benefits to regularly speaking multiple languages. First, different languages connect you to different **communities**. Your native language connects you to your family and culture. Your current **community**'s language connects you with people like your teachers and friends. Second, speaking multiple languages can benefit students learning English. They can use their native language to make sense of new words or grammar rules. For example, many languages have cognates, or words that look and sound similar in multiple languages. The English word *bicycle* is *bicicleta* in Spanish and Portuguese, *bisikleta* in Tagalog, and *bisiklèt* in Haitian Creole.

On the other hand, **constantly** switching languages might make it challenging for your brain to use one language. Andrés Ortega Cruz is from Honduras but now lives in Miami. "I switch between Spanish and English all the time," Andrés says. "I only use some words in English and others in Spanish. For example, I'll say, 'I like your *camisa* (shirt) and your *zapatos* (shoes).' But when I need to use *only* English or Spanish, it is difficult and frustrating." If you get used to switching languages **constantly**, your brain might combine, or put together, your languages instead of using them separately. This can make it harder to speak only one language at a time.

Sometimes, friends who know the same languages will switch between them when they communicate.

Your brain is essential to language, and the **multilingual** brain is especially powerful. It is more **flexible** and can **manage** multiple languages. How do you use your languages when you speak?

Close Reading

RESPOND TO SECTION 1

Reread Section 1 with a partner. Then answer the questions.

1. What is the main idea of this section?

A. Some people are multilingual.

B. Being multilingual changes how the brain works and manages languages.

C. Languages compete inside your brain.

D. A long time ago, scientists thought the brain kept languages in different parts.

2. What are two key details in this section?

A. Multilingual people have flexible brains.

B. There is no limit to how many languages you can learn.

C. Over time, your brain eventually learns how to manage multiple languages.

D. Sometimes it can be hard to say a word in English.

RESPOND WITH EVIDENCE

Use the frames to write a response. Include text evidence and precise words.

◎ Grammar Target
Don't forget! Add –<u>s</u> to a **present-tense verb** when the subject is a singular noun. *The brain **work<u>s</u>** in many different ways.*

Language to COLLABORATE
What could we write? We could write _____. Okay. Let's write _____.

Verbs (action words)				
figure<u>s</u> out	learn<u>s</u>	expand<u>s</u>	get<u>s</u> bigger	store<u>s</u>
realize<u>s</u>	understand<u>s</u>	fight<u>s</u>	compete<u>s</u>	processe<u>s</u>

How does language work inside the brain?

The brain _____ multiple languages in the same areas.
(present-tense verb: *keeps*)

Your brain _____ to make room for new languages.
(present-tense verb: *grows*)

At first, a new language _____ with your native language in your brain.
(present-tense verb: *fights*)

Eventually, your brain _____ how to manage multiple languages.
(present-tense verb: *learns*)

RESPOND TO SECTION 2

Reread Section 2 with a partner. Then answer the questions.

1. What is the main idea of this section?

A. Languages connect you to communities.

B. Constantly switching languages can cause challenges.

C. Andrés speaks Spanish and English.

D. There are benefits and challenges to switching between languages.

2. What are two key details in this section?

A. You can use your native language to make sense of words in a new language.

B. Some words have cognates in multiple languages.

C. If you constantly switch languages, your brain might combine your languages.

D. Some people in Miami speak English and Spanish.

RESPOND WITH EVIDENCE

Use the frames to write a response. Include text evidence and precise words.

🎯 Grammar Target	Language to COLLABORATE
Use **comparative adjectives** to compare two things.	What could we write?
Add **–er** to the end of the adjective: *harder* Use *more* before the adjective: *more difficult*	We could write _____. Okay. Let's write _____.

Adjectives (describing words)			Verbs (action words)	
easier	simpler	closer	blend	switch
harder	tougher	more difficult	combine	change

What can happen when you switch languages?

Using your native language can make it _____ to learn a new language.

(adjective: *simpler*)

Constantly switching languages can make it _____ to speak one

(adjective: *more difficult*)
language at a time.

If you _____ languages constantly, it can impact how flexible your brain is.

(present-tense verb: *mix*)

Speaking your native language can help you feel _____ to your family.

(adjective: *connected*)

Academic Discussion

Prompt What are the positives and negatives of using multiple languages when you speak?

💡 BRAINSTORM IDEAS

Work with a partner to write at least three ideas in each column.

🎯 Grammar Target

Don't forget! After a modal verb, use a **base verb** with no –s, –ed, or –ing endings.

I can speak English. *He might believe me.* *You should study hard.*

Positives ⊕	Negatives ⊖
One **positive** of using multiple languages when you speak is that you can _____.	One **negative** of using multiple languages when you speak is that you might _____.
• feel closer to different communities	• combine languages in your brain
• communicate with _____ _____	• struggle to _____ _____
• make sense of _____ _____	• mix up _____ _____
• teach your brain to _____ _____	• work harder to _____ _____

🔍 IDENTIFY STRONG WORDS

Review the text and lesson activities. Create a list of strong words about the topic.

	Nouns (people, places, things)	Verbs (action words)	Adjectives (describing words)
Text	• _____ • _____	• _____ • _____	• _____ • _____
Activities	• _____ • _____	• _____ • _____	• _____ • _____

EXPRESS YOUR OPINION
Rewrite two ideas using the frames.
Include strong word choices from
the word bank.

Prompt | What are the positives and negatives of using multiple languages when you speak?

Response 1

One **positive** of using multiple languages when you speak is that you can <u>feel closer to different communities.</u> For example, you can <u>communicate with teachers in English and your family in your native language.</u>

- -

Response 2

One **negative** of using multiple languages when you speak is that you might <u>have problems keeping your languages separate.</u> For example, you might <u>have a difficult time thinking of specific words in one language or another.</u>

Response 1

One **positive** of using multiple languages when you speak is that you can

_____
(base verb: *communicate* . . .)

For example, you can _____
                      (base verb: *read* . . .)

_____

- -

Response 2

One **negative** of using multiple languages when you speak is that you can

_____
(base verb: *struggle* . . .)

For example, you might _____
                       (base verb: *make* . . .)

_____

Ten-Minute Response

Prompt | What are the benefits of being multilingual?

Verbs (action words)

interact with	*to do things with others*	enhance	*to make better*
translate	*to say in another language*	appreciate	*to care about*
take advantage of	*to use to help you*	enable	*to allow*
improve	*to get better at*	contribute	*to help*

Adjectives (describing words)

confident	*know you do something well*	unique	*very special*
accomplished	*reached a goal*	helpful	*able to help*
talented	*having a special ability*	intelligent	*very smart*
impressive	*others admire you*	valuable	*important*
powerful	*have an strong impact*	desirable	*wanted*

There are many *benefits* of being multilingual. One benefit is that you can <u>appreciate other languages and cultures.</u> For example, when you speak multiple languages, you can <u>communicate with many unique groups of people.</u>

- -

There are many *benefits* of being multilingual. One benefit is that you might feel <u>impressive.</u> For example, when you speak multiple languages, you can <u>use your different languages to interact with people from many cultures.</u>

✏️ **WRITE TOGETHER**

Work with your teacher to write a ten-minute response. Include strong word choices.

There are many benefits of being multilingual. One benefit is that you can

<u>interact with people who speak different languages.</u>
(base verb: *connect . . .*)

For example, when you speak multiple languages, you can _____
(base verb: *speak . . .*)

_____

Language to COLLABORATE

What could we write?

We could write _____.

Okay. Let's write _____.

WRITE WITH A PARTNER
Work with a partner to write ten-minute responses. Include strong word choices.

There are many benefits of being multilingual. One benefit is that you

might feel _____ For example, when you speak multiple languages,
(adjective: *confident*)

you can _____
(base verb: *think . . .*)

_____

_____

There are many benefits of being multilingual. One benefit is that you can

_____
(base verb: *improve . . .*)

For example, when you speak multiple languages, you can _____
(base verb: *allow . . .*)

_____

_____

WRITE ON YOUR OWN
Write a ten-minute response on your own. Include strong word choices.

There are many benefits of being multilingual. One benefit is that you might

feel _____ For example, when you speak multiple languages,
(adjective: *special*)

you can _____
(base verb: *appreciate . . .*)

_____

_____

Listen Up!

LISTEN AND RESPOND

Listen to the presentation and look at the image. Then write and present a summary.

Reprinted from Neuropsychologia, Volume 98, K. K.Jasińska, M. S. Berens, I. Kovelman, L. A. Petitto, Bilingualism yields language-specific plasticity in left hemisphere's circuitry for learning to read in young children; Pages 34–45, 2017, with permission from Elsevier. https://doi.org/10.1016/j.neuropsychologia.2016.11.018

Language to COMPARE

My question is similar to yours.

My question is similar to (Name)'s.

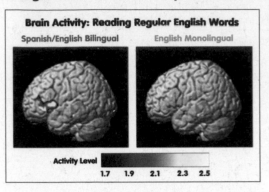

Brain Activity: Reading Regular English Words

Spanish/English Bilingual   English Monolingual

Activity Level

1.7   1.9   2.1   2.3   2.5

Key Terms

active (adj)	doing things that use energy
bilingual (adj)	speaking two languages
competition (noun)	when two things compete
monolingual (adj)	speaking only one language
retrieve (verb)	to find and then select

Summary: Brain images demonstrate that there are significant differences between

_____ and _____ brains. For example, when
(adjective)   (adjective)

reading English words, the bilingual brain is more _____ Images show
(adjective)

the bilingual brain works harder to _____ the meanings of
(verb)

words. This is because there is _____ between the two languages.
(noun)

Listen to the conversation and take notes. Then answer the questions.

Who is speaking?	What are they talking about?

1. What is Maya doing?

   A. She is participating in class.

   B. She is switching languages.

   C. She is talking on the phone.

2. What does Mason think Maya should do?

   A. He thinks she should use more Spanish.

   B. He thinks she should listen more in class.

   C. He thinks she should speak only English.

3. One question I have for Maya is: _____

_____

Speak Your Mind

LISTEN AND TAKE NOTES

Listen to the conversation again. Take notes below.

	Maya	Mason
Opinion	Maya believes that	Mason believes that
Reason	One reason is that	One reason is that
Evidence	For example,	For example,

WRITE A SPEECH

Write an opinion speech. State your claim and include a reason and evidence.

I believe Maya _____ use both languages in class, because it
(should/should not)

_____ affects her learning. One reason is that she can _____
(positively/negatively)   (base verb . . .)

_____

For example, she can _____
(base verb . . .)

_____ As a result, I believe

that Maya _____ continue to use both languages in class.
(should/should not)

Speaking at an Appropriate Pace

When you share your ideas, speak at an appropriate pace. Make sure that you:
- speak slowly
- stop to breathe
- pause to emphasize a point
- avoid using words like "um," "so," or "like"

PRESENT IDEAS

Take turns rehearsing your opinion speech. Restate your partner's opinion to show you are listening actively and carefully.

Language to RESTATE

So you think that _____?

Yes, that's right.

No, I think _____.

Present-Tense Verbs

Using Present-Tense Verbs

Writers use **present-tense verbs** to state the topic, facts, and details in an informative text. Most present-tense verbs change form depending on the subject.

After *I, you, we, they,* or a **plural noun**, use the **base form** of the verb.	After *he, she, it,* or a **singular noun**, add **–s** or **–es**.
• *I* **speak** *many languages.*	• *She* **speaks** *many languages.*
• *You* **speak** *many languages.*	• *He* **speaks** *many languages.*
• *We* **speak** *many languages.*	• *It* **speaks** *many languages.*
• *They* **speak** *many languages.*	• *Sanaya* **speaks** *many languages.*
• *Multilingual students* **speak** *many languages.*	• *A multilingual student* **speaks** *many languages.*

IDENTIFY VERBS

Draw a box around present-tense verbs. Circle the subject.

1. Your brain processes new information.

2. Multilingual students communicate in multiple languages.

3. When you learn a new language, your brain becomes more flexible.

4. Adán communicates with his family in Spanish, but his friends talk to him in English.

WRITE PRESENT-TENSE VERBS

Complete each sentence with the correct form of the verb in parentheses.

Language to COMPARE/CONTRAST
My answer is similar to (yours/<u>Name</u>'s).
My answer is different from (yours/<u>Name</u>'s).

1. Your brain _____ to manage different languages. *(learn)*

2. Your new language _____ with your native language when you learn a new language. *(compete)*

3. Some students _____ both languages to help them in class. *(use)*

4. Mika _____ speaking Japanese with her sister. *(enjoy)*

5. Languages _____ opportunities to connect with people. *(create)*

Sentence Fix-Ups

Dina and Omar are working together. They both speak Spanish. They are both new students. Dina is ask Omar in Spanish if he know what the sentence means. Omar know more English, so he help Dina.

EXPAND AND EDIT

The sentences below have two errors. Correct the sentences and rewrite them.

1. Dina is ask Omar in Spanish if he know what the sentence means.

_____

_____

2. Omar know more English, so he help Dina.

_____

Combine the two sentences into one sentence.

3. They both speak Spanish. They are both new students.

_____

_____

Look at the picture. Write a sentence about what will happen next.

4. _____

_____

Student Writing Models

What is an Informative Paragraph?

An **informative paragraph** presents ideas and information about a topic.

A The **introductory sentence** includes the topic and states the main idea.

B **Detail sentences** give facts and details about the topic.

C The **concluding sentence** restates the topic and main idea.

MARK THE PARAGRAPHS
Read each paragraph with a partner.

- Put brackets around the introductory sentence.
- Circle four present-tense verbs.
- Underline three detail sentences.
- Star five strong word choices.

Language to REACT

One new fact I learned is _____.

I was surprised that _____.

I enjoyed how the writer _____.

EXAMPLE 1

Language and Identity
By José Lemus Cruz

A Language is an essential part of a person's identity. One way language is essential to identity is that it allows people to maintain connections to their family's heritage. For example, people **B** can participate in their family's culture and traditions when they speak their family's language. Another way it is essential is that a person's name can have a significant meaning in their language. For instance, if someone's name means "peace," this might strongly impact how they feel about **C** themselves. For these reasons, it is clear that language is important to a person's identity.

EXAMPLE 2

The Brain and Language
By Somin Jung

A When you learn multiple languages, your brain changes in many impressive ways. One way your brain changes is that it adjusts to the needs of your new language. For example, your brain grows to make room for your new language. An additional way your brain changes is that it becomes **B** more flexible. For instance, your brain eventually learns how to manage switching between **C** languages. In conclusion, being multilingual can affect your brain in many fascinating ways.

Organize an Informative Paragraph

Prompt: How does your brain change when you learn multiple languages?

💡 BRAINSTORM IDEAS

Use the organizer to plan your informative paragraph.

Write an introductory sentence.
When you learn multiple languages, your brain changes in many ____impressive____ ways. (adjective: *interesting*)

What facts or details will you include?	
One way your brain changes is that it adjusts to the needs of your new language. For example, your brain grows to make room for your new language.	An additional way your brain changes **is that it** becomes more flexible. For instance, your brain eventually learns how to manage switching between languages.

Write a concluding sentence.
In conclusion, being multilingual can ____change____ your brain in many fascinating ways. (base verb: *modify*)

Write an introductory sentence.
When you learn multiple languages, your brain changes in many _____ ways. (adjective: *remarkable*)

What facts or details will you include?	
One way your brain changes is that it For example, your brain	An additional way your brain changes is that it For instance, your brain

Write a concluding sentence.
In conclusion, being multilingual can _____ your brain in many fascinating ways. (base verb: *change*)

Informative Writing

✎ **WRITE TOGETHER**
Write informative paragraphs using the frames below.

EXAMPLE 1

Language and the Brain

When you learn multiple languages, your brain changes in many

_____ ways. One way your brain changes is that it
(adjective: *incredible*)

_____ in certain areas. For example, your brain adds the new
(present-tense verb: *expands*)

language to specific _____ of the brain. Another way your
(plural noun: *regions*)

brain changes is that it figures out how to _____ multiple
(base verb: *control*)

languages when you _____ For instance, your brain learns how
(present-tense verb: *speak*)

to _____ words in the language you need. In conclusion,
(base verb: *retrieve*)

being multilingual can _____ your brain in many fascinating ways.
(base verb: *impact*)

EXAMPLE 2

Being Multilingual Changes the Brain

When you learn multiple languages, your brain changes in many

_____ ways. One way your brain changes is that it
(adjective: *incredible*)

_____ For example, your brain
(present-tense verb: *adjusts . . .*)

_____
(present-tense verb: *learns . . .*)

Another way your brain changes is that it _____
(present-tense verb: *becomes . . .*)

_____ For instance, your brain _____
(present-tense verb: *manages . . .*)

_____ In conclusion,

being multilingual can _____ your brain in many fascinating ways.
(base verb: *affect*)

Prompt: How does your brain change when you learn multiple languages?

✏ WRITE ON YOUR OWN

Write an informative paragraph. State the main idea and provide facts and details about the topic. Include present-tense verbs and strong word choices. Check your grammar and spelling.

Language to REACT

One new fact I learned is _____.

I was surprised that _____.

I enjoyed how you _____.

Title: _____

Author: _____

_____

_____

_____

_____

_____

_____

_____

_____

_____

_____

_____

ACADEMIC GLOSSARY

A glossary is a useful tool found at the back of many books. It contains information about key words.

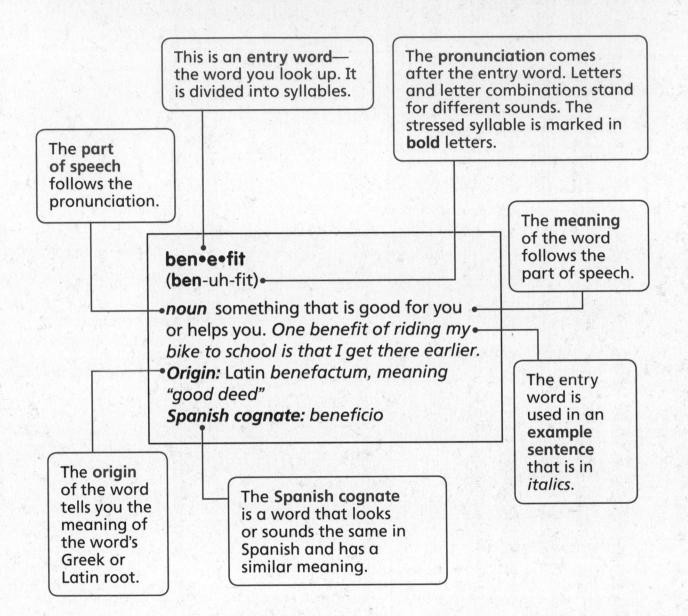

This is an **entry word**—the word you look up. It is divided into syllables.

The **pronunciation** comes after the entry word. Letters and letter combinations stand for different sounds. The stressed syllable is marked in **bold** letters.

The **part of speech** follows the pronunciation.

The **meaning** of the word follows the part of speech.

ben•e•fit
(**ben**-uh-fit)
noun something that is good for you or helps you. *One benefit of riding my bike to school is that I get there earlier.*
Origin: Latin *benefactum, meaning "good deed"*
Spanish cognate: beneficio

The **origin** of the word tells you the meaning of the word's Greek or Latin root.

The **Spanish cognate** is a word that looks or sounds the same in Spanish and has a similar meaning.

The entry word is used in an **example sentence** that is in *italics*.

a•ffect
(uh-**fekt**)
verb to change someone or something. *Hearing my favorite song positively affects my mood.*
Origin: Latin *afficere*, meaning "to influence"
Spanish cognate: afectar

ben•e•fit
(**ben**-uh-fit)
noun something that is good for you or helps you. *One benefit of riding my bike to school is that I get there earlier.*
Origin: Latin *benefactum*, meaning "good deed"
Spanish cognate: beneficio

chal•lenge
(**chal**-uhnj)
noun something that is difficult. *If you stay up late, it can be a challenge to get up the next morning.*

cog•nate
(**kog**-neyt)
noun words from different languages that look and sound similar and have similar meanings. *There are many cognates between Spanish and English, such as "cognate" and "cognado."*
Origin: Latin *co-*, meaning "together with" + *natus*, meaning "born"
Spanish cognate: cognado

com•bine
(kuhm-**bahyn**)
verb to put together. *When I bake a cake, I have to combine many different ingredients.*
Origin: Latin *com-*, meaning "together" + *bini*, meaning "two together"
Spanish cognate: combinar

com•mu•ni•cate
(kuh-**myoo**-nuh-kate)
verb to share information or ideas with other people. *My friends use texting to communicate quickly.*
Origin: Latin *communis*, meaning "shared"
Spanish cognate: comunicar, comunicarse

com•mu•ni•ty
(kuh-**myoo**-nuh-tee)
noun a group of people who live in the same area. *I look forward to the festival that our community has every summer.*
Origin: Latin *communis*, meaning "shared"
Spanish cognate: comunidad

com•pete
(kuhm-**peet**)
verb to try to do better than others at something. *Some schools have teams that compete against each other in different sports.*
Origin: Latin *com-*, meaning "together" + *petere*, meaning "aim at, seek"
Spanish cognate: competir

con•nec•ted
(kuh-**nek**-tid)
adjective feel close to someone or something. *I feel connected to my family in Ghana when we text often.*
Spanish cognate: conectado(a)

con•stant•ly
(**kon**-stuhnt-lee)
adverb describes when something always happens. *My dog constantly wants to eat human food instead of dog food.*
Spanish cognate: constantemente

cul•ture
(**kuhl**-chur)
noun the way of life that a group of people share. *Ms. Hayes taught us about the culture of the Aztecs.*
Spanish cognate: cultura

dis•con•nec•ted
(dis-kuh-**nek**-tid)
adjective feel far or distant from someone or something; not connected. *I feel disconnected from my cousin in Peru when we go too long without talking.*
Spanish cognate: disconectado(a)

dom•i•nant
(**dom**-uh-nuhnt)
adjective most common. *The dominant language in my community is Spanish.*
Spanish cognate: dominante

em•bar•rassed
(em-**bar**-uhst)
adjective when others make you feel bad about yourself. *Alex felt embarrassed when he slipped and fell in the cafeteria.*

en•cour•age
(en-**kur**-ij)
verb to tell someone to do something. *Teachers often encourage their students to do their best work and think of new ideas.*
Origin: French *en-*, meaning "in" + *corage*, meaning "courage"

ACADEMIC GLOSSARY

es•sen•tial
(uh-**sen**-shuhl)
adjective very important. *It is essential to eat healthy foods and exercise regularly.*
Origin: Latin *essentia*, meaning "necessary"
Spanish cognate: esencial

e•ven•tu•al•ly
(ih-**ven**-choo-uh-lee)
adverb at a later time. *It might take me a while, but I will eventually finish reading this long book.*

flex•i•ble
(**flek**-suh-buhl)
adjective able to change or do different things. *Sometimes I have to be flexible with my schedule when my plans suddenly change.*
Origin: Latin *flexibilis*, from *flectere*, meaning "to bend"
Spanish cognate: flexible

fu•ture
(**fyoo**-cher)
adjective coming after the present time. *In the future, some people think there will be flying cars.*
Origin: Latin *futurus*, meaning "going to be, yet to be"
Spanish cognate: futuro(a)

gen•er•a•tion
(jen-uh-**ray**-shuhn)
noun a group of people who are about the same age. *Grandchildren are the younger generation in a family.*
Origin: Latin *gernerat-*, meaning "created"
Spanish cognate: generación

hon•or
(**on**-ur)
verb to show respect to someone or something. *The city will honor the mayor with an important award.*
Origin: Latin *honos*, meaning "honor"
Spanish cognate: honrar

i•den•ti•ty
(eye-**den**-ti-tee)
noun who a person is and what is important to them. *A big part of my identity is that I am a star basketball player.*
Origin: Latin *identitas*, meaning "same"
Spanish cognate: identidad

im•pact
(**im**-pakt)
noun the effect of one thing on another thing. *The decisions you make about how to spend your time can impact how productive you are.*
Origin: Latin *impact-*, meaning "driven in," or Latin *impingere*, meaning "drive something in or at"
Spanish cognate: impacto

leg•a•cy
(**leg**-uh-see)
noun the memory people have of someone's life. *The president left an important legacy because she helped a lot of people in the country.*
Spanish cognate: legado

lim•it
(**lim**-it)
noun the greatest amount or number allowed. *The speed limit on this road is 55 miles per hour.*
Origin: Latin *limit-*, meaning "boundary, frontier"
Spanish cognate: límite

man•age
(**man**-ij)
verb to have control of something. *I like to make lists to help manage my different assignments and tasks.*
Origin: Latin *manus*, meaning "hand"
Spanish cognate: manejar

mis•pro•nounce
(mis-pruh-**nouns**)
verb to say words incorrectly. *When I am learning new words, I often mispronounce them the first time.*

mon•o•lin•gual
(mon-uh-**ling**-gwuhl)
adjective able to speak only one language. *Many people in the United States are monolingual, because they only speak English.*
Spanish cognate: monolingüe

mul•ti•lin•gual
(muhl-tee-**ling**-gwuhl)
adjective able to speak more than one language. *My cousin is multilingual because she speaks Spanish, Korean, and English.*
Origin: Latin *multi-*, meaning "many" + *lingua*, meaning "language"
Spanish cognate: multilingüe